Rachel Whiteread

Lisa G. Corrin, Patrick Elliott and Andrea Schlieker

Scottish National Gallery of Modern Art *Edinburgh*

Serpentine Gallery *London*

Published by the Trustees of the National
Galleries of Scotland with the Serpentine
Gallery for the exhibition *Rachel Whiteread* held
at the Serpentine Gallery, London from 20 June
to 5 August 2001 and at the Scottish National
Gallery of Modern Art, Edinburgh from
29 September to 9 December 2001.

Text © National Galleries of Scotland,
Edinburgh and the Serpentine Gallery,
London, 2001

Works © Rachel Whiteread, 2001

ISBN 1 903278 22 8

Designed and typeset in Cycles by Dalrymple
Printed by BAS Printers, Over Wallop

Cover and frontispiece: details from
Untitled (Upstairs), 2001, cat.13

Foreword

Considering Rachel Whiteread's international reputation, the British public has had relatively little opportunity to see her work. Despite having been the subject of numerous exhibitions abroad, winning the Turner Prize in 1993, and representing Britain at the Venice Biennale in 1997, her solo exhibition at Tate Liverpool in 1996 has remained her only one to date in Britain. This collaboration between the Serpentine Gallery, London and the Scottish National Gallery of Modern Art, Edinburgh redresses that imbalance.

Whiteread first came to the attention of a wider audience when she showed *Ghost* – a plaster cast of the interior of a room – at the Chisenhale Gallery in London in 1990. Since then, in the UK, her work has featured in group exhibitions at the Serpentine Gallery, the Saatchi Gallery, the Royal Academy of Arts, London and elsewhere. These exhibitions have placed her within the context of her peers and, albeit somewhat involuntarily, have led to her being associated with the so-called YBA (Young British Artist) phenomenon.

Whiteread was always, in fact, a slightly separate figure. She studied at Brighton Polytechnic and the Slade School of Art and not at Goldsmiths College of Art, where so many of her contemporaries trained; she works in an essentially traditional way, using casting techniques which date back several hundred years; and she was never part of the social whirl that was the hallmark of the 1990s London art scene. But the glare of publicity fell on her when *House*, the cement cast of the interior of a Victorian terraced house, was unveiled in 1993. The ensuing furore concerning its meaning, status and destruction, generated front-page headlines and became the subject of questions in parliament. The *Holocaust Memorial* in Vienna polarised opinions to a similar extent. It would not be true to say that these controversies have happened in spite of Whiteread: it is, in fact, her unrelenting determination to stick to her principles that have ensured that these projects were realised and have given them their edge.

Since *House*, much of Whiteread's energy has gone into two public projects abroad: *Holocaust Memorial*, which, after various setbacks, was finally unveiled in October 2000, and *Water Tower*, a transparent resin cast of its namesake that was erected on the roof of a high-rise building in New York in 1998. However, in 2001 Whiteread's focus has moved back to Britain, resulting in a series of casts made in a former synagogue in East London that is being converted into the artist's studio and living quarters, and *Monument*, her proposal for the vacant Fourth Plinth in Trafalgar Square. We are especially pleased to be able to present two of the new works cast in the synagogue, *Untitled (Upstairs)* and *Untitled (Cast Iron Floor)*: these were cast from the upper staircase and the terracotta floor in the synagogue, and were finished earlier this year. Playing on the difference in the two Gallery spaces, *Untitled (Upstairs)* will be shown in a vertical position in London, and horizontally in Edinburgh. *Untitled (Cast Iron Floor)* is the first of Whiteread's floor pieces, that invite direct audience participation, to be shown in the UK. These new works are presented with others dating back as far as 1988, the year Whiteread began making casts of everyday household objects such as tables, beds, baths and bookcases. While sharing the same method of manufacture, being mostly negative casts, their diversity vividly demonstrates Whiteread's relentless interest in form, process and material.

We would like to thank Rachel Whiteread for the time and consideration she has given to this exhibition and to the completion of new work, particularly while involved in preparations for the erection of *Monument* in Trafalgar Square. We are also grateful to the artist's assistants, Carolina Grau, Myron Allen, Phil Brown, Paul Carter, Alex Dexter, Katy Dexter, Jay Hall, Ian Lander, Tim Maslen, Jerry McGettrick, Andy Price, Frank Reid and David Ronalds. Special thanks also to Marcus Taylor.

As ever, we are particularly grateful to the lenders to the exhibition who agreed so readily to part with their works. We would also like to thank Anthony d'Offay and his gallery staff, in particular Susanna Greeves whose assistance has been absolutely invaluable, and also Jennifer Thatcher and Zoë Morley.

The exhibition was selected by Lisa Corrin, Chief Curator at the Serpentine Gallery, and Patrick Elliott, Curator at the Scottish National Gallery of Modern Art, in close consultation with the artist. We would also like to thank Andrea Schlieker, formerly of the Serpentine Gallery but in recent years involved in international public art projects, including *Holocaust Memorial*, for her insightful essay on Whiteread's public sculptures. We are grateful to Robert Dalrymple for designing this catalogue and to Christine Thompson for overseeing its production.

The Serpentine Gallery is delighted to collaborate once more with Bloomberg, who are the sponsors of the exhibition in London, and whose generosity has proved crucial in bringing these works to the Serpentine. We would also like to express our gratitude to The Henry Moore Foundation for their financial support.

Finally, we would like to thank all our colleagues for their efforts in making this exhibition a success. We would like to thank Richard Calvocoressi, Director of the Scottish National Gallery of Modern Art, for making this partnership possible, and also express our particular thanks to Achim Borchardt-Hume, Exhibition Organiser, and Mike Gaughan, Gallery Manager, Serpentine Gallery.

JULIA PEYTON-JONES
Director, Serpentine Gallery

TIMOTHY CLIFFORD
Director-General, National Galleries of Scotland

Rachel Whiteread, **Ghost**, 1990
Plaster on steel frame, 270 × 335 × 317cm
The Saatchi Gallery, London

Sculpting Nothing: An Introduction to the Work of Rachel Whiteread

PATRICK ELLIOTT

It is a very big plaster cube, composed of a number of smaller cubes stacked neatly on top of each other. It is not exactly cubic, but has ridges running along the top and bottom, panelling of a sort, raised sections here and there, and around the side there is a kind of fireplace, though the blackened hearth sticks out rather than in. The panelling indicates a door, but it cannot be opened, and there is a hole where the door-handle should be. The protruding section on the far side must be a sash-window in its recess, and the encircling ridges will be the skirting board, picture rail and cornice. All the cracks in the walls and woodwork have declared themselves in the plaster, but in negative form, standing proud of the surface. It is a room as we have never seen it before – a sealed space which cannot be entered. The air has been made solid and the walls have disappeared. It is the ghost of a room, hence its title *Ghost*, and it was made by Rachel Whiteread early in 1990.

Whiteread has been making work of this type since 1988, the year after graduating from the Slade School of Art in London. That year she made a plaster cast of the inside of a wardrobe. Almost all of Whiteread's sculptures are cast from objects relating to the human body: the spaces under chairs and inside cupboards, mattresses, baths, sinks, shelves, hot-water bottles, floorboards, rooms. They are the kind of banal, household things we use or move about in everyday – so normal and ordinary that they melt into the background and seem unlikely raw material for an artist. And yet they have an intimate bond with our private lives. In the bath we lie naked and defenceless; in bed we sleep, make love, give birth, fall ill and die; on the floor we stand, walk and live out our lives. These are the dumb, unchampioned cornerstones of life: not since Bonnard, Vuillard and Sickert has an artist moved them more effectively to centre stage.

We share ourselves with these things, both literally and metaphorically. An emptied bath carries the sloughed off skin, hair and grime from our bodies, while a stained mattress declares a range of possibilities, from sickness to passion. Closing the wardrobe door, we shut in our sweat, skin and smell. Silent witnesses to our most private and vulnerable moments, they are the things we clean, cover, close or hide when visitors call. Stains and dust signal our presence like fingerprints: they are our unwitting signatures, signs of our imperfection and therefore humanity, and Whiteread tracks them down with the determination of a forensic scientist. The things she has cast have a human scale and dimension, reflecting their function. Beds, baths and wardrobes are about the height or length of a person. The layout of a set of shelves is defined by our height and reach, while the size of a room responds to our need to move about and store our stuff. They are metaphors for our own lives and bodies; they are shadows of a sort.

Whiteread dramatises the personal life of furniture through the casting process, retaining the minutiae of surface detail. She uses plaster, rubber, resin and concrete, and has recently used bronze. She has often chosen colours which in some way match our bodies. Conversations with manufacturers of rubber have led to improbable requests: 'Try to make it the colour of piss in the morning'; 'Make it the colour of semen'; 'I want it to look like bone.' She has used dental plaster because of its pinky, flesh colour. This exactitude and determination to get the right materials typify Whiteread's approach. She is very precise about the kinds of objects she casts, making repeated visits to junk shops and salvage yards in the East End of London, where she lives. She describes these places as her sketchbooks.

Untitled (Black Bed) 1991 [cat.4] is the cast of the space beneath an old double bed. It is a dark, dusty, claustrophobic space, the sort of space a child might crawl into to hide. The four holes mark the places where the legs stood; the bow of the surface indicates long use and the weight of bodies. It was the kind of bed designed for a small living space, or a dwelling with limited access, in that it folded in the middle on hinges: one can imagine partly folding it, making it into a right angle to get it through a door in a narrow corridor. The hinged element itself was equipped with a sort of flap which would stretch to present a clean edge should the bed be stored in a folded position. It is this unglamourous, dusty pocket of material which, in reverse form, becomes the central axis of the sculpture. Turning the bed on its back, Whiteread re-upholstered

Rachel Whiteread, **Closet**, 1988
Plaster, felt and wood, 160 × 88 × 37cm
Private collection

the underside with hessian and constructed a frame around the bed, creating a space the same depth as the gap between bed and floor. In the same way that one might stuff a chicken or clean a blocked drain, she shoved her hand into the crack and filled it with dense black rubber, and then poured the rubber into the rest of the frame. Once set, the frame and parent object were removed. In negative form, the fabric pocket emerges as an erect ridge, covered with an unsavoury coating of fluff and human debris. The hessian covering has given the flat surface a suggestive dusting of hair. Working in this way, Whiteread's approach combines selection, replication, invention and artifice. It all recalls Francis Bacon's memorable remark, made in 1955: 'I would like my pictures to look as if a human being had passed between them, like a snail, leaving a trail of the human presence and memory trace of past events, as the snail leaves its slime.'

Whiteread's work of the late 1980s and early 1990s, in particular, has a strong grounding in personal experience, reflecting a middle-class childhood in London. Born in Ilford in 1963, the family later moved to Muswell Hill. She studied painting at Brighton Polytechnic (1982–5) but after the first year felt more drawn towards the sculpture department. She attended tutorials by sculptors such as Phylidda Barlow, Alison Wilding, Edward Allington and Richard Wilson (who gave a memorable session on how to make casts), among others. She went on to study sculpture at the Slade School of Art (1985–7), but even at this stage felt unsure that sculpture was her forte. At the Slade she made a few works which developed from casts of her own body: a cast of her back presented as a kind of shovel, a cast of part of her legs held together. These were small, discrete works that went on the wall or stood in the corner. Other works incorporated old, stained clothes. She describes *Closet* 1988, made the year after she graduated, as her first proper sculpture, the first work she could walk around, the first which did not seem ashamed of its own presence. It is a plaster cast of the inside of a wardrobe, covered in black felt. Whiteread has commented about the work of this period:

These were all very particular pieces of furniture – cheap post-war furniture – which I somehow wanted to immortalise, to give a kind of grandness. I was trying to make a space that I was very familiar with and that a lot of people would be very familiar with. And I have a very clear image of, as a child, sitting at the bottom of my parents' wardrobe, hiding among the shoes and clothes, and the smell and the blackness and the little chinks of light, and I was really trying to illustrate that... I was trying to make that space solid.[1]

These works of the late 1980s and early 1990s are a kind of exorcism, forcing out deeply held feelings about family and childhood, and exposing them to public gaze. They show incredible maturity for an artist who was then in her mid-twenties.

Yellow Leaf 1989 [cat.2] is the cast of the space underneath a kitchen table. Made in five separate elements, its method of construction, dismantlement and reassembly has informed much of Whiteread's later work, including *Ghost*. It is exactly the kind of Formica-topped table Whiteread's grandmother owned, the type that could be extended when the family came to tea: pull out the side flaps, insert the yellow leaf (kept in another room), snap it shut and everyone can sit down. The work is autobiographical in origin but it acquires a wider potency because it is the sort of memory with which most of us can identify. We may not be able to remember much of what our grandparents said or did, but odd things stick in our minds and come to embody a person and place: the curtain material, the high-backed armchair, the smell of stew, the ritual of the yellow leaf. The sculpture itself stands as a monument to such childhood memories and particularly to feelings of community. Whiteread's socialist belief (her father, originally a geography teacher, was active in the local Labour Party and her mother, an artist, remains so) informs these works.

Shallow Breath 1988 [cat.1], Whiteread's first bed piece, is the work which has drawn most comment in terms of a particular personal history, with assertions that it is a cast of the bed she was born on or the bed her father died upon. Neither is true, in fact Whiteread has never used furniture with a family origin: it is nearly all found in junk shops and salvage yards in the East End. It

Rachel Whiteread, **Untitled (Clear Slab)**, 1992
Rubber, 198 × 79 × 10cm
Private collection

relates instead, as the title partly implies, to her father's final illness with heart disease (he died the following year, shortly before Whiteread's first solo exhibition, when this work was first shown). It stands tall and dignified, if grim in pallor. The plaster (itself the stuff of hospitals and broken bones) emphasises fragility. Death pervades Whiteread's work, and she acknowledges that it is a subject she has thought a great deal about, and did so even as a child. She also acknowledges the impact two television documentaries made upon her. One reported the death of an elderly man, alone in his flat in Hackney, and the discovery of his body two weeks later (a blind neighbour was alerted by the smell). By that time the body had partly dissolved into the bed. The mattress was put outside for collection, but it remained there for several days: viewers saw children happily bouncing about on it. Another documentary concerned the removal of ancient lead coffins from a church in Spitalfields, London, and the fear that the liquid remains, still sloshing about inside, might harbour plague. One can see elements of a theme which recurs in Whiteread's work: an almost scientific interest in the trace left by a body and an obsession with the specifics of place and community (both films were shot near the artist's home). When Whiteread made *Ghost*, it was no accident that she selected a derelict house in Archway Road, North London, close to the place where she grew up, or that *House* (see pp.59–60) was made about a mile away from her own house, and was situated on a road she regularly travelled along. Offers to have *House* wheeled away to save it from demolition were firmly rebutted: it was specific to a particular place. Putting it somewhere else would have been like pretending to be someone else.

Whiteread's interest in the remains of death manifested itself in a series of works based on ceramic mortuary slabs. In 1991 she purchased a pair of these slabs from an architectural salvage yard in Hackney. From these she cast two thin, tongue-like forms in translucent orange resin which lie directly on the floor. She also made transparent rubber casts, which lean against the wall. Human in scale, these rubber sculptures have the same physical presence and

dead weight as a body. Their surfaces bear the trace of the surgeon's knife as it exited the corpse and carried through to the white ceramic top, wounding it, as it were. You could see these works as modern *memento mori*. This may sound morbid, but they are very beautiful, haunting objects, and there was an element of comedy in their making:

When I came to make these casts I didn't use a parting agent to release the rubber from the mould as it would have interfered with the detail of the surface of the piece. The nature of the process created suction and we literally had to wrestle to part the piece from the mould. It was like an enormous tongue. So there we were, dealing with an object on which people had been laid out and cut up and then having this extraordinary physical experience wrestling with it.[2]

Untitled (Pair) 1999 [cat.12] likewise derives from a mortuary slab. One of the parts presents a lightly hollowed surface, designed to capture bodily fluids and channel them towards the foot end. The second part is a cast of that same concave surface, turned upside down so that it forms a convex shape, this time bordered by a narrow lip which skirts the edge of the form: here the fluids would trickle into a groove which is bordered by the raised edge. The pair of sculptures are, so to speak, male and female mortuary slabs which would lock tightly together should one be turned upside down and placed upon the other. As with the casts after beds, these works simultaneously refer to sexuality and death. There is even something sexual in the very act of casting, in which a positive and negative form fit snugly together to produce a new thing.

Many of Whiteread's works have this dual, apparently paradoxical aspect, in that they seem domestic, comforting, nostalgic even, and yet at the same time there is something alien and sinister about them. A bath has associations with warmth and relaxation, but doubles visually as a coffin or sarcophagus. The dark spaces under beds and inside cupboards are good hiding places, but is the hiding a matter of fun or fear? *Untitled (Airbed II)* 1992 [cat.5] is cast from a blow-up lilo, the kind one might use as a spare bed for overnight guests, but it has the unmistakable look of enlarged intestines. Looked at in a certain way, a

Rachel Whiteread, Untitled (Torso), 1992–5
Plaster, 15 × 30 × 20cm
Private collection

wardrobe can seem like an imposter in the home, standing in the corner of the bedroom like a stranger. It houses a space we do not really know and do not care to investigate. Nowhere is this ambiguity more apparent than in Whiteread's casts after hot-water bottles. A hot-water bottle is something we cling to for warmth, security and comfort, yet its cast resembles nothing other than a headless, limbless child. Like the best surrealist art, it is simultaneously the stuff of dreams and nightmares. Such paradoxes lie at the heart of Whiteread's work. Her sculptures appear to represent the thing from which they are cast, but in most cases represent the very opposite. They represent the air underneath or inside or in front of a thing – everything but the thing itself. She deliberately confuses the issue by making her negative casts the same depth as the original object. So the mattresses are cast to the same thickness as the original, and Whiteread's recent negative floor, cast from terracotta floor tiles, *Untitled (Cast Iron Floor)* [cat.14], is just a centimetre thick, like the tiles themselves. However, some of the works have gone through a double casting process, to produce duplicates. Some of the beds, *Untitled (Airbed II)* [cat.5], for example, are made as plaster casts, which in turn act as the moulds to recreate the original object (or at least the front of it), but in another material. It is an upside-down, inside-out process which is difficult to follow and is fraught with almost metaphysical contradictions.

Whiteread's sculpture deals obliquely with social issues, but it is not social history, and making it work in sculptural terms is the principal aim. One can see that she is dependent upon the formal language of 1960s American minimalist sculpture, and also acknowledges British sculpture of the previous generation. At the Slade in the mid-1980s she made regular visits to London galleries. During these years Antony Gormley was making casts of his own body, presenting them as lead casings; Tony Cragg and Bill Woodrow were using household junk, including furniture, as the raw material for their work; and Alison Wilding was making seemingly abstract sculptures which have an enigmatic connection with the human form (after graduating,

Whiteread worked as Wilding's assistant for a year). One could also mention the pavement casts of the Boyle family and the early work of Richard Long, for example the photographic works in which he presents his own trace in the form of a worn patch of grass. Whiteread's sculpture contains clear references to the minimalist art of figures such as Richard Serra, Donald Judd and Carl Andre. Like their work, hers is architectural in form, it commands space, and is not plinth-based. Yet in another sense her work is the exact opposite of theirs. Instead of being abstract and emotionally aloof, Whiteread's sculpture is grounded in the faithful description – copying even – of specific objects, and through this implies some sort of narrative. Also, while the Minimalists rejected the personal inflections which so characterised the art of the previous generation (the gestural brushstroke, the vigorously modelled surface), preferring something more clinical, Whiteread carefully preserves the human mark. It is not her own mark but an accumulation of marks made by other, unknown people. In this way her work carries a communal signature as much as a personal one.

In October 1993, following two years of planning, fund-raising and negotiation, Whiteread made a cement cast of the inside of a terraced three-storey house in the London borough of Hackney. She was awarded the Turner Prize the following month. *House* was demolished, amidst great controversy, in January 1994. Within the space of a few months Whiteread had become an international media figure, shoved unceremoniously into the spotlight. At around this time, her attention shifted from casting domestic furniture to utilising standard objects such as office desks. These austere, unforgiving forms had a history too. In 1992–3 she lived in Berlin on a DAAD artists' scholarship, and this took her, in every sense, into foreign territory, away from family, friends and the familiar junkyards which had furnished her with her raw materials. She continued to cast ordinary objects (*Untitled (Concave and Convex Beds)* [cat.6] was made in Berlin) but they tended to be objects which had less personal history attached to them, simply because her own personal history lay elsewhere. Some of the works from this

Rachel Whiteread, **Untitled (Room)**, 1993
Plaster, 275 × 300 × 350cm
Museum of Modern Art, New York

period are invented rather than cast from specific objects. This is true of *Untitled (Room)* 1993, a stark, cell-like room, which makes *Ghost* look positively cosy by comparison. Two large casts of the underneath of floorboards, made at around the same time, were also invented spaces, not maps of specific rooms. From about this time Whiteread was required to attend meetings, particularly in connection with *House* and later the commission to make the *Holocaust Memorial* in Vienna. The scale and ambition of these projects, and above all the political wrangling which they generated, led to countless meetings in which committee tables – of exactly the kind she began casting – loomed large. She made a number of grey plaster casts after anonymous office desks at this time, linking them together to form unbreachable rows. Instead of bearing the warm marks

of use, they are bleak, brutal things – quiet indictments of bureaucratic mores. This has been the principal shift in Whiteread's work in the past six or seven years. Instead of focusing on personal, domestic spaces, she has become more concerned with institutional spaces. In tandem with this, her work has acquired greater formality and a certain toughness.

Whiteread's fossilised bookshelves grew out of her work on the *Holocaust Memorial*, a commission awarded by the city of Vienna at the beginning of 1996, although the work was only finished in 2000. The Viennese books have, as it were, their spines on the inside and their pages turned out towards us. The smaller, independent bookshelves are generally presented in the opposite way, indicating that we are looking at the space formerly occupied by the books. Some of these bookshelf works are stark white and regimental, the empty spaces suggesting serried volumes of the same size and possibly content. Others have a more human dimension. In *Untitled (Novels)* 1999 [cat.11] the books – or rather their spaces – show greater variety in terms of shape, order and presumably character. The pastel colour of the pages has transferred to the plaster, to create a painterly band of stripes. The difference between the two types of work is like the difference between a photograph of troops from the Red Army and those long-format school photos showing scores of pupils assembled together in wiggly lines. In this

14

way, the bookshelf sculptures elaborate upon the human metaphor so vividly embodied in the earlier bed, bath and table pieces.

Photography holds an important place in Whiteread's work and her early work, in particular, carries something of the nostalgic feel of old family photographs of friends and relatives who have died. She has a huge archive of documentary images, taken by herself or cut from magazines, and for years she went everywhere with a camera, taking photos of junk on street corners, buildings, cemeteries and so on.

Just as her sculptures are seemingly unmediated casts, in which the touch of the artist's hand is absent, so photographs can avoid the expressive gesture. Photographs, like her casts, fix an actual moment eternally in the present. They preserve the moment the shutter clicked, the moment the plaster encountered its mould and solidified. It is freeze-dried reality, the real reflected light and the real physical imprint of something, and this makes it quite different from painting, modelling or carving. It is the same unmediated reality we see in the cast corpses from Pompeii, and this is why they so fascinate us. Whiteread has exhibited her photographs alongside her sculptures, has included them in books, and has used them as the basis for screenprints. Her series of twelve photo-screenprints entitled *Demolished* were made around the same time as *House* (but were published some time later) and show East End tower blocks in the process of demolition. In the same way that Whiteread's negative casts suggest the ghostly trace of the human body without actually describing it, so the photographs of the tower blocks denote the countless lives that have been lived within them. The destruction of the tower blocks alludes to death as much as it does to social regeneration. They are memorialised buildings, and like memorials the images record loss while at the same time preserving memory.

Whiteread initially trained as a painter and something of the painter remains in her work. Her subject matter is the natural territory of painters or documentary film-makers rather than sculptors (one cannot imagine Auguste Rodin, Henry Moore or Richard Serra sculpting a bed or a wardrobe, but Van Gogh certainly painted them). Her drawings are normally made using correction fluid, a painterly, liquid medium, which behaves and even looks like plaster. She considers her coloured bookcases, stained with the edges of science fiction novels, as her watercolours. Her work is shot through with colour and is rarely ever white. While Whiteread has ordered specific colours for her rubber casts, her resin colours are a by-product of the casting technique, associated with the chemical process rather than with added pigmentation. *Table and Chair (Clear)* 1994 [cat.8] is an early resin work (the first, a

cast of a floor, was made in 1992). The impulse to use transparent resins came from the desire to show something of the interior of the object. It is a sculpture of nothing (the underside of a table and chair) so the resin material seemed a logical choice. The horizontal strata reveal the casting process, as layers of liquid resin were poured into the mould, an inch at a time to prevent cracking. It is not immediately apparent in the photograph of this work, but the chair section fits into the table, and can slide right under it. Whiteread sees it as 'a kind of doorway, a pause between inside and out' – a phrase Henri Matisse or Robert Motherwell might have used to describe their concerns in painting.[3]

The surfaces of other works have been given additional colouring. *Yellow Leaf* was smeared with cooking oil to give it a used look, but again it was an appropriate material, given the origins of the table. The stains on her mattresses are not necessarily stains transferred from the mattress itself but accidents associated with the casting and the removal of the mould. The stark grey concrete surface of *Holocaust Memorial*, meanwhile, is awaiting its additional colouring. It could have been given a paint-

resistant varnish, but Whiteread sees the grime and possible graffiti which it may attract as a logical and meaningful part of the work. She is intimately involved in the production of each piece, going to great lengths to find the right materials (one dense rubber was ordered from a firm in Germany which makes skateboard wheels; others were tracked down to a supplier in Cardiff) and testing and adapting them herself. It took a year to solve technical problems associated with the casting in clear resin of *Water Tower*, commissioned for a site in New York in 1998, and similar problems dogged the production of her transparent plinth, made in 2001 for Trafalgar Square in London. In her public sculptures she has achieved the unlikely paradox of making public monuments of a private character. In the Trafalgar Square work, *Monument*, she has, almost literally, turned the notion of public sculpture inside out and on its head. In a brilliantly observed reference to the bombast of so much public sculpture, here the plinth celebrates itself, gazing like Narcissus at its own watery reflection. It subverts and inverts the expected in a surprising yet logical way. It shows the beautiful, invisible reality of space.

15

1. Interview with Lynn Barber in *The Observer*, 1 September 1996.

2. Interview with Andrea Rose in British Pavilion, XLVII Venice Biennale, *Rachel Whiteread*, 1997, p.34.

3. *Ibid.*, p.33.

above: Rachel Whiteread, **Untitled** from **Demolished**, 1996, from the portfolio of twelve duotone screenprints, each 48.9 × 74.4cm
Scottish National Gallery of Modern Art, Edinburgh

right: Rachel Whiteread,
Untitled (Collected Works), 1998
Plaster, polystyrene and steel, 116 × 284 × 30cm
Private collection

Rachel Whiteread, **Untitled (Ten Tables)**, 1996
Plaster, 72.5 × 293.5 × 478cm
Yale Center for British Art, New Haven, Connecticut

A Conversation with Rachel Whiteread, March 2001

LISA G. CORRIN

Rachel Whiteread's sculptures are indices of human presence or absence. Cast in the negative from beds, baths, sinks or hot-water bottles, to name just four sources, her works reveal traces of our humanity and the passage of time, and, most profoundly, the cold fact of our mortality.

Whiteread begins with the most human of spaces, the house and its contents, but what results are studies in the manipulation of process, material, form, surface, mass and the productive tensions that she engenders between them. Our physical relationship to Whiteread's work inflects and compresses the experience of our physical relationship to our environments. Our perception of reality is corroborated through our bodily experience of it. Publicly-sited works such as *House* 1993 and *Holocaust Memorial* 2000 strike an eloquent equipoise between the politics and poignancy of the sites and the relentlessness of the imposing physical objects she places within them.

Increasingly, works Whiteread conceives to be seen in a gallery setting have become more and more confrontational, like *House*. Tough, massive and geometrically-driven works such as *Untitled (Ten Tables)* 1996, the centrepiece of her presentation at the Venice Biennale in 1997, or the recent *Untitled (Basement)* and *Untitled (Upstairs)* [cat.13] might even be called aggressive. I spoke to the artist just as she completed the latter two pieces, both cast from staircases in an old synagogue in Bethnal Green. The following conversation took place on 20 March 2001 and focuses on the new works she has created using this space as her source and that were, in part, the occasion for this exhibition in London and Edinburgh.

LISA CORRIN: At the Serpentine Gallery, we decided to put five works which had beds as their sources in one space. We believed that rather than looking at a room of mattresses the stark context of those white walls would emphasise that these sculptures are experiments in form, texture and cast material. They are emphatically not representations of mattresses. They occupy the space outside the space of the literal. We saw this as a means to emphasise their essential sculptural qualities and also as a way of establishing a sense of continuity with your new works. Recently, you have had a number of commissions enabling you to work on ambitious, monumental projects. Consequently, your primary interest in mass has been inflected and your continued investigation of material and process on an exceptionally large scale has, more than ever, resulted in works which bear comparison with those of sculptors of a previous generation, such as Richard Serra, Mark di Suvero, Donald Judd, Carl Andre and Eva Hesse.

Untitled (Basement) especially reminds me of the index-less, industrially fabricated works of Judd. Its coldness fits my idea of Rachel Whiteread as a hard-edged abstractionist at heart. Its forms are detached from their original relationship to a staircase. Although it shows the process as all of your work does, it is 'cleaner', more geometric, less referential. It is much farther removed from its relationships to a staircase than *Untitled (Upstairs)*. In its upright orientation, *Untitled (Upstairs)* still retains its specificity. It walks a much tauter tightrope between the literal and the non-representational.

There are other stark differences between these two works. The patina of *Untitled (Basement)* is clinical, smooth and bears less of the signs of the cast tearing away from the surface of the original form. It is not quite slick, but the process by which it was made seems almost industrial. I associate the heavy patination on *Untitled (Upstairs)* with the suggestive surfaces of old things. It is what makes people fetishise antiques. I guess I feel that the more your work can be fetishised or anthropomorphosised the farther we get from understanding it in terms of sculpture in dialogue with its inherent historical references and the language of art making.

18

Rachel Whiteread, **Untitled (Upstairs)**, 2001, cat.13, and details of the staircase in Rachel Whiteread's studio from which **Untitled (Upstairs)**, was cast.

The forms of *Untitled (Basement)* are dense, impossible, puzzle-like, even perverse. *Untitled (Upstairs)* is precariously balanced, but feels, ironically, less massive. I wouldn't call it ethereal exactly, but it suggests a stairway to nowhere. There is a strong sense of upward movement.

RACHEL WHITEREAD: *Untitled (Basement)* is much more polite in its objectivity. *Untitled (Upstairs)* works differently, and I think it's partly due to the volume and the height, and being able to actually walk underneath it. But I also feel that it does something uncanny. It inverts your sense of place. It is almost like some of my very early pieces and the way they surprise people by turning the world inside out, which is what I understand people found so arresting. I think that *Untitled (Upstairs)* has done exactly that. It is to a large degree due to its scale. There is confusion about its relationship to the original stairs. You have this awkward lump which is sort of

sticking up. I find it an incredibly uncomfortable, powerful and strange object, and I'm still trying to figure out why.

LC: *Untitled (Upstairs)* changes with each site. You will be reorienting it to respond to the spaces of the Serpentine Gallery and the Scottish National Gallery of Modern Art in Edinburgh. At the Serpentine it will be seen upright and will play off the height of the architecture of the domed space. In Edinburgh, where it cannot fit upright, you have decided that it would work equally well on its side.

RW: I always thought about the context of the staircase pieces, that they would have to relate to the architecture. I felt they should be reoriented, if need be. I had to take into consideration the exhibition of *Untitled (Basement)* at three different branches of the Guggenheim – in Berlin, Bilbao and New York. I had reservations for various reasons, but then I started to think about the architecture of the three

Rachel Whiteread, **House**, 1993
193 Grove Road, London E3, destroyed 1994
Photo: John Davies

Guggenheims. I tried to make a work that would be about the architecture of the Guggenheim because that is what the Guggenheim is – buildings. I spent ages trying to think about this, and went and looked at them, and I thought this is just crazy; what I need to do is bring my architecture to them. I can't play with their architecture, it has to be the other way around, which is what made me think about the staircases. I was very excited about the possibility of the staircase that worked with the apartment I had cast and that could completely reorient and change the emphasis of the show, just by tipping the staircase over, whichever way it might fit in the room with the other piece. So it was really about being able to play with these elements.

After casting the staircases I felt very strongly that *Untitled (Upstairs)* was the one that should exist on its own as a singular piece of sculpture. It is rare that I make models for sculptures, but the staircase pieces were originally made as 1:10 scale models – playful objects in my studio – which made it easier to decide upon the orientation of the works.

In Edinburgh, turned on its side and placed centrally in the room, *Untitled (Upstairs)* will be like a puzzle. But I am not trying to make an Escher drawing in which you have this annoying psychological game where you're trying to traipse your way around one of his drawings. For me it is primarily a physical experience.

At the Serpentine Gallery, *Untitled (Upstairs)* will fit against the wall, but there is going to be a space behind it, so one can walk underneath it. It's going to seem gargantuan. I wanted to make something that was more resistant than *Untitled (Basement)* and I think a bit more aggres-

sive; something that could really stand alone in that space.

LC: And stand up to that space? To do something to it? So from many points of view the piece takes up something that wasn't possible in *House*.

RW: Right.

LC: The way in which the viewer negotiates each piece will be very different. You have always been sensitive to the 'approach' to a work as critical to its experience. The movement towards the work is as significant as the movement around the work.

RW: With *House*, it was a very strange sensation walking down the street, half a mile away, knowing that you were coming up to it, seeing this great green plinth – the grass around it. Suddenly there was this monolith. You couldn't help but be in awe of this massive, bizarre object that fucked up everybody's perception of their home, their houses, their domestic life, and their 'safe' places.

LC: Was it your interest in movement that led you to make the staircase pieces?

RW: As an undergraduate, I studied painting, though I wasn't very disciplined about the edges of a canvas – everything always ended up as three-dimensional drawings, drawings you could walk through and around. In retrospect I think I was dealing with, even then, what I understood to be 'invented space'.

LC: How is the way in which you have produced the new pieces different from *House*?

RW: *House* was a continuation of my early work from the late 1980s, like *Yellow Leaf* 1989 [cat.2] and *Closet* 1988, where elements of the originals became an integral part of the work. When making *House* we cast a concrete skin throughout the whole building – casting around the wooden stairs and floors.

LC: You can 'read' the stairs as a zigzag in photographs of the side of *House* since you cast around them.

RW: That's right. More recently with the staircase pieces and new pieces based on the cast of an apartment, the investigation

19

Rachel Whiteread, **Untitled (Bronze Floor)**,
1999–2000, 98 units, 1 × 350 × 700cm
Courtesy of the artist and Anthony d'Offay Gallery, London

has become more rigorous. The walls have been removed and the spaces re-articulated. All has been stripped down and revealed. I think the movement and physicality is an inherent part of these works.

In order to make the staircase pieces we had to think very carefully about the mould work. Unlike *House* where the mould was literally demolished, in this case each individual piece had to be considered and removed from the mould – a very complicated process. The release agent worked to varying degrees and this is what determined the surfaces of the pieces. I always try to be honest about the way a sculpture is made, its geometry, where spaces start and where they end; all of these decisions have to come into play at the mould-work stage. I have to be able to visualise the completed sculpture as a 'whole'. I make informed decisions based upon my experience, but I'm usually happy to embrace surprises. Actually, I started thinking about making staircases back in 1993, but I suppose it was with the recent pieces that I started thinking about them with some degree of sophistication.

LC: One of the exciting things about your sculpture is that it is full of contradictions. It plays with pressure points, weights and

balances, and something appears to be one thing and it's really something else. Surely the viewer's perception of the balance within the piece will vary with its siting. Although it will be on its side, I think, ironically, that sense of intentional imbalance will be more in evidence. Can *Untitled (Upstairs)* stand upright, without being attached to a wall?

RW: It could do, by weighting it. I would not have wanted to bolt it to the floor, but I don't want to be in any way responsible for a personal injury by making a large piece of work that could possibly fall over. So I felt far more comfortable, especially within somewhere like the Serpentine, about it leaning against the wall.

LC: I am interested in the element of threat. It does, of course, raise the spectre of Richard Serra. I hadn't thought about physical threat in relation to your work but rather psychological threat. The minute the object is removed from its context, as in the case of *House*, it immediately becomes a bit unnerving. When you go one step further and turn it on its side, you have a vague recollection of the source, in some part of yourself it resonates. Yet it isn't itself. It is its negative and this creates a wrenching feeling in the gut. In contrast, *Untitled (Bronze Floor)* 1999–2000, the piece for the Haus der Kunst in Munich, still retains its essential character as a floor. You invite the viewer to walk on it.

RW: They are having a new museum built. So what I decided to do was to take a fingerprint from the old museum and then transfer that to the new museum. So we went over and cast an area that was essentially the size of the skylight that was above it.

LC: So that the floor literally related to the ceiling?

RW: The original is a stone floor from the mid-1930s that has been worn, with little mishaps from over the years appearing on the surface. We cast the floor in plaster and then translated it into bronze. The patina is white and comes from applying a chemical and wax. When the piece is finally placed back in the new museum visitors will walk across it. All of the pieces that are now in positive, which

Carl Andre, **144 Magnesium Square**, 1969
Magnesium, 1 × 366 × 366cm
Tate, London

are all the areas that were in negative on the original floor, are now slightly raised. In a few years time new traces will be apparent on the piece where the patina has been worn away, adding another dimension to the work.

LC: How do the floor pieces you are currently doing relate to the staircase pieces?

RW: They relate to the staircases because they are also pathways. They are thoroughfares, they are about walking over something, about what our presence actually does to a surface. They may look like Carl Andre, very tough, minimal blank tiles, but there's a whole other type of activity that is going to shape what happens to these, that might take some time, but changes will happen. This is exactly the same type of floor piece that I'm doing in the exhibitions at the Serpentine and in Edinburgh.

LC: You can also walk on Andre's pieces. What makes yours different?

RW: Sure you can walk on his pieces, but they're not patinated in a way that will really change in the course of time.

LC: Carl Andre's works do change colour, but you're talking about a different kind of change.

RW: When people walk across my piece I think it can be compared to making a painting or drawing. My floor piece consists of hand-cast and patinated elements that were painstakingly made. This is always the case with my work; I try to make something look effortless and it becomes an intensive process. All of the little bits of history that have happened to the floor – where someone's been up a ladder and dropped a hammer, or a tile has had to come up for some reason and then has been put down and shattered – all of those experiences remain on the surface of the piece and will become even more apparent as the public walks over it.

LC: A crucial component of the piece is not just the beauty of its economic form, but also that its history continues to unfold, indeed, come to light as part of the act of continual making precipitated by the public's interaction with the piece. They are polishing the negative impressions of history, as it were.

RW: I think this relates to the *Holocaust Memorial*. When I was thinking about that piece and the place where it was going – Vienna – I was also thinking about this floor piece, which is in Munich in an extraordinary mid-1930s building. It, too, has certain overtones of a particular time in German history. I think the political elements of the site which it was intended to occupy came into play as I conceived it.

The *Holocaust Memorial* has certainly informed my way of thinking about things over the years.

LC: Can you relate the floor piece for Munich to the one you're doing for this exhibition?

RW: After making the Munich piece I had the opportunity to work in the building where my new pieces have been made. It is a disused synagogue that for fifteen or twenty years was a textiles warehouse. There is this incredible sense of history within the building. It's in Bethnal Green, East London, which is the heart of what was the Jewish community in that part of London. This particular synagogue was originally a Baptist church. It has this kind of strange history to it, and when I started thinking about the building, which is a building that I am eventually going to be living and working in, I was combing every surface of it thinking about how we would change it to house the studio and meet my needs for both working and living. But I was also combing the surfaces for its history. I wanted to map the building. I feel delighted that I've been able to make these works. If I should change the building enormously I would have a record of its past. Whether the pieces end up in Europe or America or in storage in my studio, it's satisfying to have made these impressions of a building that I am probably going to be involved with for the rest of my life. I've never really done that before. Whenever I make a piece, the original objects are essentially destroyed. Making the apartments, making the staircases and then making these floor pieces, it's like making a series of prints.

LC: Why did you feel strongly about starting the exhibition at the Serpentine with the floor piece?

RW: Fourteen years ago I worked as a gallery assistant at the Serpentine. I was struck by the Serpentine Gallery's audience, always a great mixture of art aficionados and recreational members of the public who stroll into the gallery quite unintentionally. I wanted the first gallery to initially seem empty, so that the piece was walked upon before it was noticed, acting as an unexpected introduction to the exhibition. I may put it quite close to the entrance, so you really do just walk in and on it.

LC: That would make it most un-Carl Andre like, because his work is very detached. Although in principle it is supposed to violate museum protocols, visitors often aren't aware that they have a choice to walk upon it. In my experience it's very rare to see somebody walk across a Carl Andre work. People tend to be reverent because it looks so intentionally like 'art'.

RW: I certainly wanted to make something that was very discrete, but also confrontational.

LC: That perhaps defines what you're trying to do in your work in general.

RW: I think it probably does. This piece is only a centimetre high and it's black and the floor is grey.

LC: That is pretty discrete.

RW: But when you walk across it, some of the tiles are slightly wobbly. When you're on the piece it is a bit uncomfortable and there's nothing else on the walls.

LC: That will certainly disturb a visitor's sense of security. But then that is what an art gallery should do, isn't it – dislodge our expectations. Can you describe the surface of the piece? How will that add to the experience of the work?

RW: The piece is made from cast iron that has been patinated. There's not much daylight in the room where it will be installed, but the surface will be slightly reflective. Light breaks across the surface, and it almost disappears even though it's a solid mass. The surface is incredibly fragile not in terms of the cast iron as a metal, but fragile in terms of its ability to absorb human activity as a printing process.

LC: The test piece for the work is very atmospheric. It's almost like a storm cloud, very ominous and at the same time it looks quite insubstantial. It's strange when you think about how heavy this material is. The surface is sensual. There are these wonderful ripples and edges to it.

RW: The ripples around the edges are from the original grouting. Many of these pieces were sent back to the foundry to be recast;

if some of the surface detail is missed it can look smudged, like a badly proofed print.

LC: Looking at the cast iron sample, which is black, makes me think about your judicious use of colour in your work. You felt strongly about having a room of mostly black works in the exhibition. The black bed in the exhibition also has raised indentations along the centre, and almost looks like an elongated version of this tile. Of course it's made of an entirely different material. It's made of rubber.

RW: Actually it's a foundry casting rubber. It was made during a period when I was really pushing materials and trying to stretch them beyond their limits.

LC: Why?

RW: I'm incredibly interested in materials. I'll pick something up and be very curious about how it has been made. I then begin on research and development and get a bit caught up with it and I find that I am trying to do something that no one's ever done before. A lot of money, and an awful lot of heartache later may lead to something incredible. I'm interested in the science of materials. Not in their chemical making, structures and molecules, but in how materials have developed and how and why we use them. There are some amazing man-made materials out there. I recently realised when I was walking in the country that I was wearing Gore-tex on my feet, as a jacket and in my mouth, through the wonders of modern dentistry. Quite an extraordinary twentieth-century material.

LC: But to return to the colour black, you have repeatedly employed it throughout your career, from your earliest work to the elegant shelf of black books which you made in 1997.

RW: Black is inert. In my mind, the first true sculpture that I ever made was *Closet* 1988. I had previously made a lot of things that flopped on the floor or leaned against something, and they didn't really stand on their own two feet. So eventually when I left college I made *Closet*, which is black. Originally *Closet* was about trying to make a childhood experience concrete: I came to it from that angle. I was trying to think of a material that was as black as childhood darkness, which is fundamentally frighten-

ing because you don't know what's in that darkness. I was trying to use a material that would suck the life out of light. I looked at various things and black felt seemed to be the right material.

The use of felt was also partly informed by my memory of sitting inside wardrobes. As a child, I used to sit in wardrobes. My parents had this wardrobe that was full of clothes and boxes full of fabric. You could be in this place that was incredibly comforting and dark, totally surrounded by material. There would be a little chink of light, but essentially it was black, and it was totally enveloping. I wanted to make that experience tangible, that's sort of where that thing came from.

Later on, with *Untitled (Black Bed)* 1991 [cat.4], the second black piece that I made, I used a material that I could smear. This wasn't necessarily why I used it, but when I started to make this piece, the material was very viscose and you had to spatula it onto the surface of the side of the bed that I was 'casting'. There's a kind of ridge running across the centre of it. I remember a friend of mine described it as resembling something you'd find underneath your fingernails, which I thought was a wonderful description of this piece of work, just this sort of 'uh, what's that?' Or, I remember someone else describing it as the sort of fluff that you find inside your pocket. *Untitled (Black Bed)* was part of an ongoing investigation I made with beds. I suppose if I had made *Closet* later on there would have been many versions of it, as the investigations can be intense.

LC: So that is why there are so many works based on a bed in different materials. You did a number of baths and they took many different forms, and each one is very distinct.

RW: I originally made three plaster bath pieces that were all cast from different baths. And three that were all poured out of one mould, though they're all made from different materials. One is yellow, one is amber and one is black. The black one is made from yellow plastic which I dyed black. I very rarely dye a material. Even though these are all made of plastic and rubber they were the most elemental of the pieces I've done. The yellow piece was very like beeswax or lard. The orange

23

one was very like amber, but it was also cast in such a way that it was like a tectonic plate, or resembled the way in which sediment settles. *Untitled (Black Bath)* 1996 [cat.9] was like coal. When I was making it I don't think I was necessarily conscious of that: I find these things out once I have made them. Once I had all three of them in the studio, I thought they related to landscape, which is also something that I think has happened with the book pieces that I've made more recently.

LC: How so?

RW: Well, if you look at the edges of the books, especially at the top where a lot of them have colour, they're really like cliff faces. This is a very literal way of seeing them. However, I do find it interesting how some of these works remind me of landscapes. When I was a student in Brighton and had first started painting, I worked with landscapes for two years. Over the past twelve years I think all of these experiences have been filed together as a language that I've developed, whether it's come from American art of the 1960s or from British sculpture from the generation previous to mine such as the work of Alison Wilding, Richard Deacon or Tony Cragg. They all got knitted together and inform how I work.

LC: To describe them as landscapes is very literal. In fact, it reminds me that your early works had titles that were also concrete and referential.

RW: The titles were poetic, very scripted. But then I stopped because I felt the titles gave far too much away, which is why the new pieces have only a bare-bones description, e.g., *Untitled (Upstairs)* and *Untitled (Basement)*.

LC: In the new works, you've chosen to give a title that retains the context of the piece, its sense of place. The context shapes your approach to the making of the work. Isn't that close to being site-specific? And yet in the case of the publicly-sited pieces such as *Water Tower* 1998 in New York or *Monument*, your project for Trafalgar Square, which is currently in process, they are both made of near-transparent materials that can blend into their surroundings.

RW: The piece for Trafalgar Square is discrete. Both there and not there.

LC: *Water Tower* has been acquired by the Museum of Modern Art in New York which suggests that it is not exactly site-specific. Isn't there an incredible irony in a work being commissioned by the Public Art Fund and then winding up inside a museum?

RW: No, I don't think so because I think *Water Tower* was made for a site, but it was also made for New York. There are water towers throughout the whole of New York, and the water tower that was actually cast on top of that building wasn't the original water tower from that building, it was taken from somewhere else. Someone wanted to buy it and take it to Los Angeles and I said no. If it's going to stay somewhere, it needs to stay in New York. I also didn't mind if it went inside. This was long before I'd even put it on the roof, but I kept thinking, 'wouldn't it be fantastic if having lived outside, there came a point where it might need to go inside?' When you see the piece in a room, it's enormous. But when you see it outside, it's absolutely tiny, just like a little gem on the horizon. I liked the idea of playing with scale.

With the plinth in Trafalgar Square I've always assumed that it is going to stand in Trafalgar Square for probably six months or a year. Then we're going to build another stone plinth and it's going to go somewhere else. I really don't mind that, because there are plinths all over the place. It's not about the plinth actually going in Trafalgar Square, it's about the monument. I've responded to the meaning of the place and it has been part of the genesis of these works.

LC: Richard Deacon once said to me that you are the most interesting sculptor working today who is dealing with mass. You know exactly how to make something so massive seem so light ... Eva Hesse comes to my mind, particularly when I think of this quality in your work.

RW: I was very interested in Hesse when I was an undergraduate. I started thinking about her incredibly fragile fibreglass pieces that you can walk through, pieces that run along the floor and hang from the ceiling. She used transparent and fragile

Rachel Whiteread, **Study for 'House'**, 1992/3
Correction fluid on laser copy, two sheets,
overall 60 × 42cm
Courtesy of the artist

Rachel Whiteread, **Sketchbook November 1994**
Ink and correction fluid, 17.8 × 10.3cm
Courtesy of the artist

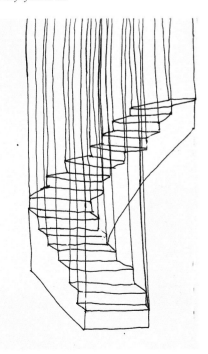

materials with a very feminine quality. I remember similar works by Robert Morris, but they were much more robust, weren't they? Her pieces were very much drawn from inside of her. I don't think it was necessarily because she was a woman, but I think her work had an incredible vulnerability.

LC: Drawing was really key to Hesse's work. It is also important to you. You keep a special space in your studio for drawings and I am always fascinated when I come here by the way they are hung on the walls. You are, by your own admission, somewhat obsessive. While waiting, sometimes years, to realise a major work, such as the stairway or floor pieces and *Holocaust Memorial*, you make highly abstract drawings that repeat the essence of the sculptural form that is gestating almost as a way to maintain your patience. These private works on paper and in your notebooks provide a unique insight to how once a form gets firmly lodged in your mind as an idea for a piece, it is nearly impossible to dislodge it. It is fascinating to look, for example, at John Davies's photograph of *House* seen from the side alongside the early drawings of pathways and staircases in your notebooks and then look at your two new works.

RW: For ten years I've been doing virtually the exact same kinds of drawing and I keep on doing it.

LC: Some of them are sketches in small notebooks. You showed me some staircases from the early 1990s, for example. Others are more fully realised like watercolours and collages using correction fluid. There is a lot of repetition, skewed grids and herringbone patterns that look like floors. They are quite uneven and far from meticulous.

RW: That's intentional. I sometimes look away from the drawings whilst I am making them, playing with an element of chance. I also make other drawings that are meticulous. It depends on my mood.

LC: They are not all abstract patterns.

RW: I have drawings that were done before *House* was realised that are very architectural. I began doing them in 1991.

LC: What's interesting also is that you've framed the drawing from your own painted backdrop and it's a room. It's a house that looks as though the plaster has been poured in between the walls of the room. This is like a drawing of what a child thinks Rachel Whiteread's *House* must have looked like and how it must have been produced. There's nothing diagrammatic about it. You also made photographic collages. There is one based on photographs taken of Hoxton Square which date from before *House*.

RW: It was done in 1992.

LC: You used correction fluid to cover the building. Were you thinking about *House* already?

RW: When I made this I was looking for a building, and I think it might have even been before I spoke to Artangel about making *House*. I lived around Hoxton at that point and was looking for places to make a piece of work. I was thinking about trying to make something that wouldn't necessarily require me to destroy the house. I had the idea of making the piece and moving it. I didn't know that I could ever have the possibility of destroying a building in the cause of sculpture.

I thought about it very obsessively. I would take these photographs and then look at them at home and fantasise about making it. So that was the function of all these drawings.

LC: It still sustains you when you have no idea how something will ever get realised. The staircase project has been gestating for ten years even before you made *House*. *House* was a real turning point in your work. Are the new works in Bethnal Green another turning point?

RW: I feel that right now I've got to a certain place with the work. *Holocaust Memorial* has finally been completed and the plinth for Trafalgar Square is well underway. I think it's a kind of transition in my work and probably in my life as well.

List of Works

1 **Shallow Breath** 1988

Plaster and polystyrene
185 × 90 × 20cm
Private collection

2 **Yellow Leaf** 1989

Plaster, formica and wood
73.7 × 150 × 94cm
Fundação Calouste Gulbenkian / CAMJAP, Lisbon

3 **Untitled (Amber Bed)** 1991

Rubber
129 × 91.5 × 101.5cm
Collection Carré d'Art – Musée d'Art Contemporain de Nîmes, France

4 **Untitled (Black Bed)** 1991

Fibreglass and rubber
30 × 188 × 137cm
Collection Irish Museum of Modern Art, on loan from the Weltkunst Foundation

5 **Untitled (Airbed II)** 1992

Polyurethane rubber
122 × 197 × 23cm
Tate. Purchased with assistance from the Patrons of New Art through the Tate Gallery Foundation 1993

6 **Untitled (Concave and Convex Beds)** 1992

Rubber and neoprene
Two parts: 34 × 100 × 196cm;
40 × 100 × 196cm
Goetz Collection, Munich

7 **Untitled (Wardrobe)** 1994

Plaster and glass
180 × 125 × 46cm
Private collection Anne Faggionato

8 **Table and Chair (Clear)** 1994

Resin
69 × 102 × 75cm
Private collection

9 **Untitled (Black Bath)** 1996

Pigmented urethane and urethane filler
80 × 207 × 110cm
Private collection, London

10 **Untitled (Black Books)** 1997

Black plastic, foam and steel
30 × 101 × 23cm
Private collection, London

11 **Untitled (Novels)** 1999

Plaster, polystyrene and steel
121 × 163 × 26cm
Astrup Fearnley Collection, Oslo

12 **Untitled (Pair)** 1999

Bronze and cellulose paint
Two parts: 89.8 × 77.1 × 204.1cm;
90 × 77 × 204cm
Scottish National Gallery of Modern Art, Edinburgh. Purchased with assistance from the National Art Collections Fund 2001
Exhibited in Edinburgh only

13 **Untitled (Upstairs)** 2001

Mixed media
320 × 780 × 410cm
Courtesy of the artist and Anthony d'Offay Gallery, London

14 **Untitled (Cast Iron Floor)** 2001

Cast iron and black patina
1 × 502 × 411cm
Courtesy of the artist and Anthony d'Offay Gallery, London

1   Shallow Breath 1988

3   Untitled (Amber Bed) 1991

6   Untitled (Concave and Convex Beds) 1992

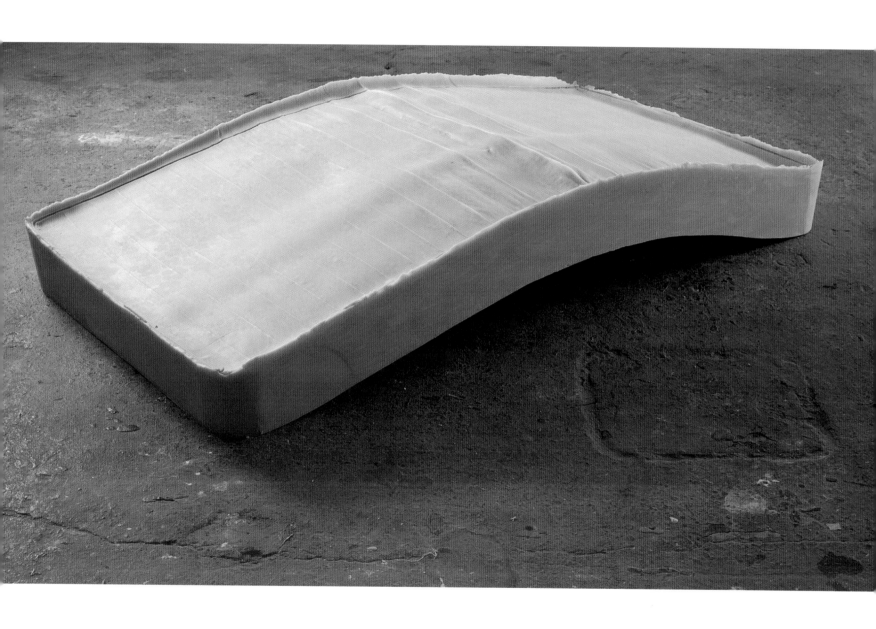

7   Untitled (Wardrobe) 1994

12   Untitled (Pair) 1999

14   Untitled (Cast Iron Floor) 2001

Pause for Thought: The Public Sculptures of Rachel Whiteread

ANDREA SCHLIEKER

Rachel Whiteread's name is still inseparably linked with her first public commission, the now legendary *House* 1993, a cast of the complete interior of a building in London's East End. Although it had a lifespan of no more than two and a half months and was made when the artist was only thirty years old, *House* has become a benchmark of twentieth-century public sculpture. Over the next six years, three other extraordinary public commissions were to follow, in New York, Vienna and London, all of which confirm Whiteread's singular talent and rare sensitivity in handling the complexities of public space.

By 1993 Whiteread had established herself as a major player on the international museum circuit. But success in the museum does not necessarily guarantee the successful handling of a public work. To operate outside the safe four walls of a Gallery requires completely different skills in an artist. As Daniel Buren, the French conceptual artist and *éminence grise* of public sculpture, pointed out:

> *Art in the street? Why not?! But only if it is rethought, revised and reorientated. It would be a mistake to suggest that there is a kind of equality between the museum and the street. They have little in common. And a lot of differences ... The point is that the unlimited freedom given to the artist in the museum no longer obtains in the street ... The point is that in the city, politics and economics are involved in everything.*[1]

Whiteread certainly came to experience those concerns most acutely, yet refused to be defeated by administrative restrictions and political wrangles.

In spite of their formal and material differences, the four commissions made between 1993 and 2001 – *House, Holocaust Memorial, Water Tower* and *Monument* – are connected by Whiteread's particular ability to elicit the poetic from the ordinary and familiar, to give form eloquently to both personal and collective history, as well as by her astute understanding of the specifics of site. All of the sculptures share a sense of subtle genealogy and logical development.

Rachel Whiteread, **House**, 1993
193 Grove Road, London E3, destroyed 1994

House

193 GROVE ROAD, LONDON E3, 1993

Solidifying and actualising emptiness, *House* was an extension of Whiteread's earlier cast of the interior of a Victorian living room, *Ghost* 1990, which had heralded her international reputation. In turn, *House* can be seen as a formal and conceptual stepping stone towards the evolution of her *Holocaust Memorial* in Vienna. Covering every corner, wall, staircase and window with (sprayed) concrete and then peeling away the actual 'skin' of the building, *House* became a life-size, negative mirror image of the intangible, air-filled spaces that were once inhabited. No one who saw *House* will ever forget its extraordinary impact: the shock of the blind windows with their powerful crosses, of an ordinary, private home literally petrified and turned inside out, of perceiving life transformed into a kind of fossil which, like archaeologists, we had to decipher.

Whiteread deliberately chose a modest Victorian terraced house, so quintessentially British, for her first public commission:[2] 'It makes a point about the smallness and fragility of the spaces we actually live in, worry about, and feel secure inside.'[3] This relationship to our direct domestic environment and its emotional resonance is of course characteristic of all of Whiteread's work. Equally striking is the formal reference *House* makes to the tomb or mausoleum, a leitmotif that started with *Ghost* and was to find its most powerful incarnation in the Vienna memorial.

Though *House* has long disappeared, its ghost still clings to the location in Bow today. Once a rough, working-class area, this East End borough has been gradually gentrified over the last few years. Part of a row of condemned buildings, Whiteread's *House* was the last one left standing and thus she deliberately foreshadowed the changing history of this part of London. Four years later her *Water Tower* was to be an equally elegiac symbol for the shifting identity of New York's SoHo district,[4] the artistic community of which, once so central to this part of town, has recently been deserting it for the more fashionable area of Chelsea.

From its inception, *House* was engulfed by huge public controversy, mainly driven

59

Rachel Whiteread, **Holocaust Memorial**, 2000
Judenplatz, Vienna
Concrete, 3.8 × 7 × 10m

60

by a few local residents and one outraged councillor. Although the work was always conceived as a temporary piece, the artistic community, realising its extraordinary potential, fought passionately to prolong its life, even gaining support from the House of Commons.[5] Yet all efforts failed and *House* was finally demolished in January 1994. Permanence was not to be granted to her work until six years later, with the commission for the Holocaust memorial.

Holocaust Memorial

JUDENPLATZ, VIENNA, 2000

In January 1996 Whiteread emerged as the winner of a prestigious international competition for the design of a Holocaust memorial in Vienna's Judenplatz, the city's old Jewish centre, with the proposal of an inverted library.[6] Like *House*, *Holocaust Memorial* became embroiled in a maelstrom of highly charged debates that cut right across Austria's political and religious landscape, thwarting progress for four years until the memorial was finally unveiled in October 2000. Whiteread commented on the relationship between the two works: 'The difference between *House* … and the Judenplatz monument is

that *House* was in effect a private sculpture being made public "by default" (as a result of its scale and visibility). The Judenplatz monument is from inception bound up in history and politics.'[7]

The small and intimate scale of Judenplatz seemed to offer a perfect foil for Whiteread's artistic approach. Unlike other squares in the city, many of them major tourist attractions displaying the grandiose and heroic order of much metropolitan city planning, the Judenplatz, although central, appears hidden away, almost domestic. For an artist who quarries notions of interiority with such determination and poetic clarity it was crucial for her conceptual development of the memorial that Whiteread should perceive the square itself, so tightly packed with houses on all sides, as a kind of interior or room, the streets leading into it as doorways.[8] The strong geometrical order of the surrounding façades, with their rusticated ground floors and horizontal cornice lines, became a vital visual marker to underpin the grid-structure of Whiteread's emerging plan. At the same time, the artist was struck by the predominantly residential nature of the square. Unlike London, Vienna has managed to keep a centre that is not completely taken over by shops and offices, but instead offers its citizens an integrated living space. The rich stucco of the façades is mirrored inside the houses, where period ornament abounds in lofty rooms. Taking her cue as always from the given context, Whiteread's 'library' displays details such as a ceiling rose, cornices and panelled double doors, ubiquitous features of these nineteenth-century bourgeois interiors. Thus the typical room size of a Judenplatz apartment,[9] as well as the nature and size of the square itself, not only galvanised the conceptual process for Whiteread's work but became the benchmark for its human scale.[10]

Whiteread was familiar with the distinguishing appellation of Jewish people as 'people of the book'. According to Jewish belief, the book epitomises heritage and endurance in the face of displacement and Diaspora; it is seen as a symbol of sanctuary for Jewish learning and for the continuance of tradition. The word, rather than the image, was the central messenger for the story of Jewish suffering. In Whiteread's *Holocaust Memorial* the book is a symbol, both powerful and evocative, yet it is firmly fixed within a domestic iconography.[11] The memorial's shelves are filled with seemingly endless copies of the same book, a reference to the vast number of victims and their life stories; books now forever closed. It is an inverted and hermetic library: the books do not reveal their content and their spines remain invisible. 'Reading' the memorial becomes a claustrophobic experience, as the viewer metamorphoses into the sensed wall against which the books are pressing.[12] The double doors, offering the possibility of entering or leaving, are hermetically sealed. The void encloses an eloquent reminder of the 65,000 lives forever lost: it is the core of the work.

At once familiar and uncanny, the library appears to be exhaled from the surrounding houses. A private place for contemplation and learning, stranded in a public square, its emotional force, as always with Whiteread, is restrained, dignified, and elegiac. With its seemingly endless rows of books, of histories lived, of things said and written, and yet to be said and written, her library presages the infinite process of mourning which this memorial announces. Unlike any of her other public commissions, the Vienna memorial carries the challenge and the burden of permanence. And, also in contrast to previous work, it is not cast from a 'found' object, an existing room or situation, but is constructed entirely of elements emerging from the artist's imagination and thought.

With her library Whiteread has conceived a sculpture that is an antidote to the heroising monument.[13] Through an association of humble tomb, grand mausoleum and empty cenotaph, it commemorates and embodies loss; indeed, a memory of things now irredeemably lost resonates through all Whiteread's work. In some way perhaps, her sculptures encapsulate the quintessence of what we mean by memorial.

Water Tower

60 GRAND STREET & WEST BROADWAY, MANHATTAN, NEW YORK, 1998

Only six months after the demolition of *House* in 1994, Whiteread was approached by New York's Public Art Fund to conceive a temporary public sculpture for their city. Given a completely open brief about location and with no preconceived idea about what she might want to do, Whiteread wandered the streets of Manhattan and Brooklyn in search of inspiration. The fact that Whiteread eschewed a number of grand locations in the city – which had been offered to her – for the more modest yet potentially powerful possibilities of an ordinary brownstone's rooftop is, of course, characteristic of her quiet, restrained approach. As far as sites for public art go, this setting is perhaps the ultimate self-effacing gesture. Unlike the in-your-face quality of so much 'plaza-art', a rooftop location implies active search or accidental discovery, thereby making surprise part of the experience of looking.

The happenstance of 'finding' a water tower[14] as object of choice and mould for her sculpture, also sets it apart from her projects in Judenplatz and Trafalgar Square, where location was given. Cast in four-and-a-half tonnes of clear polyurethane resin, Whiteread's *Water Tower* was installed on top of a vacant 'dunnage' (their metal support structure), in June 1998.

As an object, *Water Tower* has the same succinct aptness and resonance as *House*. Both have iconic status for their particular socio-cultural and national contexts, both are relics of a past that is about to disappear. And, like *House*, *Water Tower* was perceived to be 'so fused with the site that it becomes a fitting memorial to the neighbourhood itself'.[15] Whiteread's understanding of site-specificity, a key term in debates on public art that first emerged in the late 1960s and early 1970s,[16] converges with and yet goes beyond that of her minimalist antecedents. When it was suggested that *House* should be re-sited in Milton Keynes or when, in 1996, local residents demanded that *Holocaust Memorial* should be moved from an intimate and enclosed square to a large and open one, Whiteread's rejection was immediate and

Rachel Whiteread, **Water Tower**, 1998,
60 Grand Street & West Broadway, Manhattan,
New York
Resin, 4 × 3m

categorical. For her, the nature of the alternative sites constituted profoundly different coordinates from the ones for which the works had been conceived. 'Site-specific works deal with the environmental components of given places', the American sculptor Richard Serra famously stated. 'The scale, size, and location of site-specific works are determined by the topography of the site, whether it be urban or landscape or architectural enclosure.'[17]

Water Tower however, following its purchase, has now been relocated successfully, and with the full approval of the artist, on the roof of the café-building of New York's Museum of Modern Art. Whiteread accepted the new site as she saw that it shared the main characteristics of the original location. In accordance with a general shift in art practices over the last few decades, Whiteread's definition of the term site-specific, once held to mean forever fixed and unchangeable, no longer adheres to the narrow dictum Serra had proclaimed during the infamous *Tilted Arc* debacle – 'to move the work is to destroy the work' – but allows for a more open consideration of alternative sites, provided a similarity and affinity of their nature is guaranteed. Susan Hapgood had already observed this shift in 1990: 'the once popular term "site-specific", has come to

mean "movable under the right circum-stances"'.[18]

Apart from the marginal and ephemeral nature of the site, the utilitarian yet strangely anachronistic aspect of a wooden water tower, naturally appealed to the artist.[19] For Whiteread, always fascinated by anonymous architectural forms and their functions, *Water Tower* also relates, like all her work, to a basic human need, for example, to drink and to bathe. In an interview she said: 'I wanted to find something that was domes-tic in scale and part of the city, of its furni-ture. I started thinking about the way water towers feed buildings. They're like tear ducts of buildings.'[20] This anthropomorphisation, the equation of a building with a human organism, throws up a multitude of other associations. It emphasises once again the underlying presence of an absent body in all of Whiteread's work.[21]

At the same time *Water Tower*, a cylindri-cal container with a conical top, is reminis-cent of a large urn, just as the box-like plinth on Trafalgar Square may connote a coffin. Its discreet position fosters invisibility.

The sense of the miraculous emanates from this work as in no other of Whiteread's oeuvre. Like a transparent column of water, frozen in mid-air, it brings to mind the story of Tuccia, one of Rome's vestal virgins, who proved her chastity by carrying water in a sieve. Although Whiteread had used luminous coloured resins before, most notably in *Untitled (One Hundred Spaces)* 1995, this was the first time she had experimented with pure translucency, thereby heightening its spectral and evanescent appearance. As J.E. Cirlot remarks: 'The "state of transparency" is defined as one of the most effective and beautiful conjunctions of opposites: matter "exists" but it is as if it did not exist, because one can see through it. As an object of contemplation, it offers neither hardness nor resistance ...'[22]

What particularly fascinated Whiteread about clear resin was that it enabled her to reveal the object's interior, which in previous work had been hidden by the opacity of the material. Yet with *Water Tower* the limits of visibility are pushed to its extreme; she talks about wanting 'to break it down so it's virtually not there'[23] and 'on a cloudy, grey day ... it might just completely disappear'.[24] The process of rendering something invisible can perhaps be traced back to Whiteread's particular method of drawing, where white fluid erases the lines and shapes of a given image.

The *Water Tower's* combined vocabulary of transparency, verticality and inaccessibility further triggers thoughts about ascension, alchemy and the spirit, whilst the container itself recalls the form of the chalice, cauldron or coffer, receptacles which have always alluded to magic and the bearing of secrets. This metaphysical reading seems to be confirmed by Whiteread's own collection of visual markers which provided the diverse sources of inspiration for the making of *Water Tower*.[25] They range from images of cloud formations, icebergs, waterfalls and aqueducts to alleged photographic evidence of ghosts and ectoplasm.

Water in combination with its container is, of course, referenced in many Whiteread sculptures, most notably in her early casts of hot-water bottles and her series of baths. When she exhibited *Untitled (Resin Corridor)* 1995 at the Venice Biennale in 1997, the nine blocks of greenish-blue resin seemed like a river, its flow momentarily arrested on the gallery floor. Since, prior to solidification, all of Whiteread's working materials necessarily go through a liquid state during casting, there may also be a special affinity to the nature of water at that simple level.

Water Tower is the most ethereal of all her public works, giving the impression of a fleeting and marvellous crystallisation about to dissolve into the atmosphere.

Monument

TRAFALGAR SQUARE, LONDON 2001

Whiteread continues the theme of transparency with her project for the Fourth Plinth in Trafalgar Square. But instead of the height, airiness and verticality of her New York sculpture, her starting point in London is solid, earthbound and horizontal. The anonymous street corner has been exchanged for one of the most prominent landmarks in the world. What is immediately striking about Whiteread's design for the empty plinth is its formal symmetry and its apparent simplicity. Whiteread wants her works to look 'effortless', an organic part of the urban landscape, rather than a grand invasion by an artist's hubris. As she has remarked: 'to make something look simple is the hardest thing in the world ... I think it's about finding the right place for them as well. They have to be sitting in the right place.'[26]

Traditional casting or mould-making implies the necessary destruction of the original object. But here the original becomes integrated, *is* plinth for its upturned simulacrum. Like a transparent Siamese twin, the plinth, made of clear resin, has been merged with a doppelgänger. Resting in perfect equipoise, the sculpture's inherent dualism of light and dark, weight and airiness, the solid and the translucent, spawns further dichotomies like heaven and earth, corporeal and spiritual, obscure and lucid. The plinth, which strangely has never been occupied, was part of Sir Charles Barry's design for Trafalgar Square of 1841. There, this work continues the Victorian theme that was so central to *House*, but is also alluded to in the Viennese library and in *Water Tower*. History takes form, accumulated time becomes palpable.

A plinth of such imposing dimensions – at four and a half metres it is more than twice the height of an average person – dwarfs the spectator and demands that his gaze be lifted in an attitude of veneration. Even when not surmounted by a trium-

63

Rachel Whiteread, **Monument**, 2001
Resin, 4.5 × 5.1 × 2.4m
Trafalgar Square, London

64

phant figure, height immediately commands gravitas and pathos. Ever since Auguste Rodin, modernist sculpture has striven to eliminate the base or pedestal – now perceived as an outmoded distancing device – in order to break down the sense of hierarchy and to achieve independent sufficiency and autonomy for the sculpture. With this in mind, Whiteread's version of the plinth takes an ironic stance, deflating its former pomposity by turning it upside down and emphasising a pivotal point in the display of public sculpture. The oblong 'blockishness' of *Monument* relates this work not only to predecessors like the bath sculptures but also to *House* and the Vienna memorial. Like *Water Tower*, it is a hollow container. Its form is also reminiscent of an altar or a coffin, thereby alluding to the notion of the *memento mori* which pervades all of Whiteread's work.

To make a sculpture in such a central, noisy and bustling location, and to complement an assembly of plinths that otherwise carry the heroes of history,[27] must have been completely against the natural inclination of an artist who always strives for the intimate and silent. Her response was to create a kind of seclusion zone, a 'pause' as she put it, 'a quiet moment for the space'.[28] Like *Water Tower*, the work merges with the surrounding architecture. The horizontal cornice lines of the double plinth draw attention to the cornices of surrounding buildings, which can actually be seen *through* the sculpture.

The artist commented that *Monument* is about 'drawing people's attention to things that have been left behind. I don't really invent things, I work with the object that's there and subvert things.'[29] Yet in this apparently simple mimetic process the original object becomes transformed, the familiar is rendered uncanny.

In the act of translucent doubling, *Monument* is perhaps Whiteread's formally simplest, most pared down and most purely architectural work. The clear lines of its geometry are given greater prominence, the new height is closer to that of a cenotaph, and its cuboid form recalls the rigorous language of American Minimalism. Once again, a Victorian relic is converted into a modernist icon, a mere thing into a potent metaphor. Whiteread's public sculptures are poignant interventions in the city, prompting us to rethink our existing world, taking us on unexpected journeys.

Whiteread's long-standing fascination with architectural structures, her quiet, sure-footed approach, her fusion of the monumental and the everyday, and her sensitivity to the specifics of site, all contribute to the fact that her public sculptures – whether temporary or permanent – are now seen to be amongst the most importantly seminal in recent history.

1 Daniel Buren, 'Can Art Get Down From Its Pedestal and Rise to Street Level?', in *Sculpture. Projects in Münster 1977*, Stuttgart, 1977.

2 *House* was commissioned by Artangel and Beck's. For a full account of its genesis and the surrounding debate see *Rachel Whiteread, House* (ed.) James Lingwood, London, 1995.

3 Rachel Whiteread interviewed by Louisa Buck, 'Casting About', in *Harper's Bazaar*, June 1994, p.58.

4 See Roberta Smith, 'The Ghosts of SoHo', in *The New York Times*, 27 August 1998 and Robert Storr, 'Remains of the Day', in *Art in America*, April 1999, pp.105–8 and p.154.

5 See *Rachel Whiteread, House*, p.144.

6 For a full account of the making of this work and the surrounding debates see Andrea Schlieker, 'A Book Must be the Axe for the Frozen Sea Within us. Rachel Whiteread's Holocaust Memorial', in *Projekt: Judenplatz Wien. Zur Konstruktion von Erinnerung* (ed.) Simon Wiesenthal, Vienna 2000.

7 Rachel Whiteread, 'Statement on the Project', in *Judenplatz Wien 1996*, Vienna 1996, p.84.

8 Rachel Whiteread interviewed by David Sylvester, 'Carving Space', in *Tate: The Art Magazine*, no.17, spring 1999, p.47.

9 The memorial is 3.8m high, 7m wide and 10m long.

10 'I don't think I have made anything that hasn't been related to my own physicality, my own scale', in 'Carving Space', p.46.

11 Whiteread made a number of book-sculptures during the following years, all of which emerged, as she put it, 'through frustration with the Holocaust memorial and I think when that is made I will stop making book pieces', *ibid.*, p.46.

12 At the same time, the books of Whiteread's library make tacit reference to the excavated bimah beneath the square, the stage on which the holy book, the Torah, was once read.

13 No doubt informed by Adorno's dictum about the impossibility of aestheticising terror after Auschwitz, the so-called anti- or counter-monuments were developed by artists such as Hans Haacke, Jochen and Esther Gerz in the 1980s. For further information see Stephan Schmidt-Wulffen, 'The Monument Vanishes, A Conversation with Esther and Jochen Gerz', in *The Art of Memory. Holocaust Memorials in History* (ed.) James Young, Munich, London and New York 1994, p.69; Hans Haacke, 'Und ihr habt doch gesiegt', *ibid.*, p.77; Andrew Causey, *Sculpture Since 1945*, pp.217–27, and Christoph Heinrich, *Strategien des Erinnerns. Der veränderte Denkmalbegriff in der Kunst der 80er Jahre*, Munich 1993. Particularly interesting in

this context is also Micha Ullman's *Bibliothek 1994* in Bebelplatz in Berlin. Sunk into the ground, Ullman's library of white empty shelves makes solemn reference to the book burnings that took place in that square in 1933. Standing on a square glass plate, the viewer looks down into a void that might have been an archive for the 20,000 books that were burnt by the Nazis. For a detailed discussion see *Bibliothek. Micha Ullman* (ed.) Friedrich Meschede Verlag der Kunst, 1999. See also Horst Hoheisel's inverted fountain, sunk into the ground in his *Monument to the Aschrott-Brunnen*, Kassel, 1987, in Young, pp.36–7.

14 Whiteread settled on the location in 1996. *Water Tower* is 4m high and 3m wide. It has 8cm thick walls, is hollow inside and was cast as a monolithic form. For further information see Louise Neri (ed.), *Looking Up: Rachel Whiteread's Water Tower*, Zurich 1999.

15 See Roberta Smith, 'The Ghosts of SoHo'.

16 In particular, Miwon Kwon 'One Place After Another: Notes on Site Specificity', in *October* 80, spring 1997, pp.85–110.

17 Richard Serra, 'Tilted Arc Destroyed', in *Art in America* 77, no.5, May 1989, pp.34–47.

18 See Miwon Kwon, p.97.

19 Water towers first appeared in New York in the 1830s; there are now 17,000 water towers on New York rooftops. 'The water tower, a strictly functional item, intrudes upon the turn-of-the-millennium Manhattan with the allure of a backwoodsman at a cocktail party.' Luc Sante, *Looking Up: Rachel Whiteread's Water Tower*, New York, 1999, p.89.

20 Eve McSweeney, 'Watch this Space', in *Harper's Bazaar*, May 1999, p.122.

21 An aperture, as a kind of air hole which sometimes marks the entrance to interior ducting [like a windpipe] is present in the *Holocaust Memorial* (in the centre of the ceiling rose), as well as in the top of the *Water Tower* and in some of her casts of baths and mortuary slabs.

22 J.E.Cirlot, *A Dictionary of Symbols*, London 1983, p.74.

23 See 'Carving Space', p.42.

24 See Rachel Whiteread quoted by Molly Nesbit in *Looking Up*, p.100.

25 *Ibid.*, pp.110–37.

26 See 'Carving Space', p.42.

27 The other three plinths carry statues of George IV and two military commanders from the days of the Empire, Generals Napier and Havelock.

28 Rachel Whiteread quoted in 'Trafalgar Square Fourth Plinth', *Talking Sculpture, Sculpture at Goodwood*, 2000.

29 *Ibid.*

Biography

1963
Born London

1982–5
Brighton Polytechnic, Painting

1985–7
Slade School of Fine Art, London, Sculpture
Lives and works in London

AWARDS

1992–3
DAAD Fellowship, Berlin

1993
Turner Prize, Tate Gallery, London

SOLO EXHIBITIONS AND PROJECTS

1988
Carlile Gallery, London

1990
Ghost, Chisenhale Gallery, London

1991
Arnolfini Gallery, Bristol
Karsten Schubert Ltd, London

1992
Rachel Whiteread: Recent Sculpture, Luhring Augustine Gallery, New York
Rachel Whiteread: Sculptures, Centre Cultural, Fundacion Caixa de Pensions, Barcelona
Rachel Whiteread: Sculptures, Stedelijk Van Abbemuseum, Eindhoven

1993
Galerie Claire Burrus, Paris
Rachel Whiteread: Sculptures, Museum of Contemporary Art, Chicago
House, commissioned by Artangel Trust and Beck's, London
Rachel Whiteread: Zeichnungen, DAAD-Galerie, Berlin

1994
Rachel Whiteread: Zeichnungen, Galerie Aurel Scheibler, Cologne
Rachel Whiteread: Skulpturen/Sculptures, Kunsthalle, Basel; ICA Philadelphia; ICA Boston
Rachel Whiteread: Drawings, Luhring Augustine Gallery, New York

1995
Rachel Whiteread: Sculptures, British School, Rome
Rachel Whiteread: Untitled (Floor), Karsten Schubert Ltd, London

1996
Rachel Whiteread: Demolished, Karsten Schubert Ltd, London (in collaboration with Charles Booth-Clibborn & Paragon Press)
Rachel Whiteread: Sculptures, Luhring Augustine Gallery, New York
Rachel Whiteread: Sculptures 1988–96, Prix Eliette von Karajan, Max Gandolph-Bibliothek, Salzburg and Herbert von Karajan Centrum, Vienna
Rachel Whiteread: Shedding Life, Tate Gallery, Liverpool

1997
Rachel Whiteread, Palacio de Velázquez, Museo Nacional Centro de Arte Reina Sofia, Madrid
Rachel Whiteread, British Pavilion, XLVII Venice Biennale

1998
Water Tower, Public Art Fund, New York
Rachel Whiteread, Anthony d'Offay Gallery, London

1999
Rachel Whiteread, Luhring Augustine Gallery, New York

2000
Holocaust Memorial, Judenplatz, Vienna

2001
Monument, Fourth Plinth Project, Trafalgar Square, London
Rachel Whiteread, Serpentine Gallery, London; Scottish National Gallery of Modern Art, Edinburgh

GROUP EXHIBITIONS

1987
Whitworth Young Contemporaries, Manchester

1988
Riverside Open, London
Slaughterhouse Gallery, London

1989
Whitechapel Open, London
Einleuchten, Deichtorhallen, Hamburg

1990
British Art Show [3], touring exhibition, McLellan, Glasgow, Leeds City Art Gallery, Leeds and Hayward Gallery, London
Mat Collishaw, Hanne Darboven, Angus Fairhurst, Gunther Förg, Michael Landy and Rachel Whiteread, Karsten Schubert Ltd, London
Marina Abramovic, Kate Blacker, Marie Bourget, Angela Bulloch, Leslie Foxcroft, Paola Pezzi, Tessa Robbins, Kay Rosen, Yoko Terauchi, Marylin Weber, Rachel Whiteread, Victoria Miro Gallery, London

Rachel Whiteread
Detail from **Study for 'Floor'**, 1992
Brown ink and correction fluid
38.2 × 28.6cm
Courtesy of the artist

1991

Metropolis, Martin-Gropius-Bau, Berlin

Kunst Europa, Kunstverein, Pforzheim

Broken English: Angela Bulloch, Ian Davenport, Anya Gallaccio, Damien Hirst, Gary Hume, Michael Landy, Sarah Staton and Rachel Whiteread, Serpentine Gallery, London

Katherina Fritsch, Robert Gober, Reinhard Mucha, Charles Ray and Rachel Whiteread, Luhring Augustine Gallery, New York

Turner Prize Exhibition: Ian Davenport, Anish Kapoor, Fiona Rae, Rachel Whiteread, Tate Gallery, London

Confrontaciones 91: Arte Último Briánico y Espanol, Palacio de Velázquez, Madrid

1992

Doubletake: Collective Memory and Current Art, Hayward Gallery, London

Damien Hirst, John Greenwood, Alex Landrum, Langlands & Bell and Rachel Whiteread, Saatchi Collection, London

Documenta IX, Kassel

Contemporary Art Initiative: Contemporary Works of Art bought with the help of the National Art Collections Fund, Sotheby's, London

London Portfolio: Dominic Denis, Angus Fairhurst, Damien Hirst, Michael Landy, Langlands & Bell, Nicholas May, Marc Quinn, Marcus Taylor, Gavin Turk, Rachel Whiteread and Craig Wood, Karsten Schubert Ltd, London

Lili Dujourie, Jeanne Siverthorne, Pia Stadtbaumer, Rachel Whiteread, Christine Burgin Gallery, New York

Summer Group Show: Robert Barry, Keith Coventry, Angus Fairhurst, Michael Landy, Stephen Prina, Bridget Riley, Rachel Whiteread, and Alison Wilding, Karsten Schubert Ltd, London

Lea Andrews, Keith Coventry, Anya Gallaccio, Liam Gillick, Damien Hirst, Gary Hume, Abigail Lane, Sarah Lucas, Steven Pippin, Marc Quinn, Marcus Taylor and Rachel Whiteread, Barbara Gladstone Gallery and Stein Gladstone Gallery, New York

New Voices: Recent Paintings from the British Council Collection, Centre de Conférences Albert Borschette, Brussels

The Boundary Rider: 9th Biennale of Sydney, Sydney

1993

In Site: New British Sculpture, National Museum of Contemporary Art, Oslo

Visione Britannica, Valentina Moncada and Pino Casagrande, Rome

New Voices: Jeunes Artistes Britanniques, Musée National d'Histoire et d'Art, Luxembourg (and subsequent British Council tour until 1995)

Passageworks: Geneviève Cadieux, Lili Dujourie, Dan Graham, Asta Gröting, Gary Hill, Rachel Whiteread and Alison Wilding, Rooseum Centre for Contemporary Art, Malmö

Then and Now: Twenty-Three Years at the Serpentine Gallery, Serpentine Gallery, London

Made Strange: New British Sculpture, Museum Ludwig, Budapest

The Sublime Void: An Exhibition on the Memory of the Imagination, Koninklijk Museum voor Schone Kunsten, Antwerp

Drawing the Line against Aids, Peggy Guggenheim Collection, Venice; Guggenheim Museum Soho, New York

Whiteness and Wounds: Claudia Cuesta, Sarah Seager and Rachel Whiteread, The Power Plant, Toronto

Turner Prize Exhibition: Hannah Collins, Vong Phaophanit, Sean Scully and Rachel Whiteread, Tate Gallery, London

Junge Britische Kunst: Zehn Künstler aus der Sammlung Saatchi, Art Cologne, Cologne

Der Andere Maßstab: Skulpturen (Marcel Broodthaers, Eduardo Chillida, Barry Flanagan, Gunther Förg, Guido Geelen, Hubert Kiecol Vladimir Skoda, Rosemarie Trockel, William Turnbull, Andreas Urteil and Rachel Whiteread), Edition Sabine Kunst, Munich

A Decade of Collecting: Patrons of New Art Gifts 1983–1993, Tate Gallery, London

1994

Visione Britannica: Notions of Space (Alan Charlton, Alex Hartley, Mona Hatoum, Brad Lochore, Rachel Whiteread, Stephen Willats and Craig Wood), Gallery Bonomo, Rome

Drawings: Louise Bourgeois, Asta Gröting, Eva Hesse, Roni Horn, Kathy Temin, Rosemarie Trockel and Rachel Whiteread, Frith Street Gallery, London

Sense and Sensibility: Women Artists and Minimalism in the Nineties, The Museum of Modern Art, New York

Drawing on Sculpture, Cohen Gallery, New York

Seeing the Unseen, Nvisible Museum, Thirty Shepherdess Walk, London

Re Rebaudengo Collezione, Radiomarelli, Turin

Artists' Impressions: Richard Long, Victor Burgin, Antony Gormley, Helen Chadwick, Ian McKeever, Adam Lowe, Grenville Davey and Rachel Whiteread, Kettle's Yard Gallery, Cambridge

Art Unlimited: Multiples From the 1960s and 1990s, Arts Council Collection, South Bank Centre UK touring show

1995

Double Mixte: Générique 2 (Barry × Ball, Lynne Cohen, Pascal Convert and Rachel Whiteread), Galerie National du Jeu de Paume, Paris

Ars '95, Museum of Contemporary Art and Finnish National Gallery, Helsinki

Contemporary British Art in Print: The Publications of Charles Booth-Clibborn and his imprint The Paragon Press 1986–95, Scottish National Gallery of Modern Art, Edinburgh; Yale Center for British Art, New Haven, Connecticut

Five Rooms: Richard Hamilton, Reinhard Mucha, Bruce Nauman, Bill Viola and Rachel Whiteread, Anthony d'Offay Gallery, London

British Art of the 80s and 90s: The Weltkunst Collection, Irish Museum of Modern Art, Dublin

Contemporary British Sculpture: From Henry Moore to the 90s, Auditorio de Galicia, Santiago de Compostela; Fundaçao de Serralves, Porto

Here & Now, Serpentine Gallery, London

British Abstract Art, Part 2: Sculpture, Flowers East Gallery, London

Brilliant! New Art from London, Walker Art Center, Minneapolis; Contemporary Arts Museum, Houston

Arte Inglese: A New Generation, Galleria Maravini, Bologna

New Art in Britain, Museum Sztuki, Lødz, Poland

Prints and Drawings: Recent Acquisitions 1991–1995, British Museum, London

Carnegie International 1995, Carnegie Museum of Art, Pittsburgh

Istanbul Bienali, Istanbul Foundation for Culture and Arts, Istanbul

Prö'em: Drawings Towards Sculptures, Rubicon Gallery, Dublin

1996

Bild-Skulpturen-Bild: Neuere Aspekte plastischer Kunst in der Sammlung Jung, Suermondt-Ludwig Museum, Aachen

Ace! Arts Council Collection New Purchases, Hatton Gallery, Sunderland

Mahnmal und Gedenkstätte für die Jüdischen Opfer des Naziregimes in Österreich 1938–1945, Kunsthalle Wien, Vienna

Works on Paper from the Weltkunst Collection of British Art of the 80s and 90s, Irish Museum of Modern Art, Dublin

1997

Skulpture Projekte, Münster, Germany

Sensation: Young British Artists from the Saatchi Collection, Royal Academy of Arts, London; Neue Nationalgalerie im Hamburger Bahnhof, Berlin; Brooklyn Museum of Art, Brooklyn, New York (1999)

Art from the UK: Rachel Whiteread, Abigail Lane, Douglas Gordon, Sammlung Goetz, Munich

1998

Wounds, Moderna Museet, Stockholm

Displacements: Miroslaw Balka, Doris Salcedo, Rachel Whiteread, Art Gallery of Ontario, Toronto

Toward Sculpture, Fundação Calouste Gulbenkian, Lisbon

Real/Life: New British Art, Tochigi Prefectural Museum of Fine Arts; Fukuoka Art Museum; Hiroshima City Museum of Contemporary Art; Tokyo Museum of Contemporary Art, Ashiya City Museum of Art and History

Claustrophobia, Ikon Gallery, Birmingham; Middlesborough Art Gallery; Mappin Art Gallery, Sheffield; Dundee Contemporary Art Centre, Dundee; Cartwright Hall, Bradford

Milestones in British Sculpture, Skulptur in Schlosspark Ambras, Austria

Inaugural Exhibition, Luhring Augustine Gallery, New York

Fifty Years of British Sculpture, NatWest Group Art Collection, London

Family, Nvisible Museum, Edinburgh

Thinking Aloud, Kettle's Yard, Cambridge; Cornerhouse, Manchester; Camden Arts Centre, London

An Exhibition for Children, 242 Inc., New York

1999

Le Musée à l'heure anglaise (Sculptures de la collection du British Council: 1965–1998), Musée des Beaux-Arts de Valenciennes

House of Sculpture, Modern Art Museum of Fort Worth, Texas

Ten for the Century: a View of Sculpture in Britain, De La Warr Pavillion, Bexhill-on-Sea

2000

Sincerely Yours, Astrup Fearnley Museum of Modern Art, Oslo

Le temps vite, Centre Georges Pompidou, Paris

HausSchau – Das Haus in der Kunst, Deichtorhallen, Hamburg

La forma del mondo / la fine del mondo, Padiglione d'arte contemporanea, Milan

Shadow of Reason, Galleria d'Arte Moderna, Bologna

2001

The Language of Things, Kettle's Yard, Cambridge

Public Offerings, Los Angeles Museum of Contemporary Art

Double Vision, Galerie für Zeitgenossiche Kunst, Leipzig

Selected Publications

1991

Broken English (exhibition catalogue, essay by Andrew Graham-Dixon), Serpentine Gallery, London

Technique Anglaise: Current Trends in British Art by Liam Gillick and Andrew Renton, London and New York

1992

The Boundary Rider: 9th Biennale of Sydney (exhibition catalogue, edited by Anthony Bond), Sydney

Doubletake: Collective Memory and Current Art (exhibition catalogue, edited by Lynne Cooke and Greg Hilty), Parkett Verlag, Zurich and South Bank Centre, London

1993

In Site: New British Sculpture (exhibition catalogue, edited by Karin Hellands-jo), *Terskel/Threshold* Magazine 9, Museum of Contemporary Art, Oslo

Rachel Whiteread (interview, edited by Beryl Wright), Museum of Contemporary Art, Chicago

Rachel Whiteread: Gouachen (exhibition catalogue, essay by Friedrich Meschede), DAAD-Galerie, Berlin

Rachel Whiteread Plaster Sculptures (exhibition catalogue, essay by David Batchelor), Karsten Schubert Ltd and Luhring Augustine Gallery, New York

Rachel Whiteread: Sculptures (exhibition catalogue, introduction by Stuart Morgan, conversation with artist by Iwona Blazwick), Stedelijk Van Abbemuseum, Eindhoven

1994

House (limited edition, photographs by John Davies), Artangel Trust, London

Nvisible Museum: Seeing the Unseen (exhibition catalogue, edited by Peter Fleissig), Thirty Shepherdess Walk, London

Parkett No.42: Lawrence Weiner and Rachel Whiteread, texts by Adam Brooks, Trevor Fairbrother, Richard Francis, Daniela Salvioni, Rudolphe Schmitz, Dieter Schwartz, Neville Wakefield and Simon Watney, Zurich

Rachel Whiteread: Sculptures/Skulpturen (exhibition catalogue, edited by Thomas Kellein, essay by Christophe Grunenberg), Kunsthalle Basel, ICA Boston and ICA Philadelphia

Shark Infested Waters by Sarah Kent, London

1995

Das Schwere und das Leichte by Angela Siesche, Dumont, Cologne

Excavating the House (VHS video and audiotape, contributions from Jon Bird, Mark Cousins, James Lingwood and Doreen Massey), ICA, London

House, essays by John Bird, John Davies, James Lingwood, Doreen Massey, Ian Sinclair, Richard Shone, Neil Thomas, Anthony Vidler and Simon Watney, London

Rachel Hus by Johanna Ekstrom, Dicter, Stockholm

Rachel Whiteread: House (26 minute VHS video of the making and destruction of *House*, made in collaboration with Rachel Whiteread), produced by Artangel and Hackneyed Productions, copyright Artangel, Hackneyed Productions and Rachel Whiteread

Rachel Whiteread: Sculptures (exhibition catalogue, essay by Pier Luigi Tazzi), British School at Rome

1996

'Inside Outcast' by Mark Cousins, *Tate: The Art Magazine*, London, winter

Rachel Whiteread: Shedding Life (exhibition catalogue, essays by Fiona Bradley, Rosalind Krauss, Bartomeu Marí, Stuart Morgan and Michael Tarantino), Tate Gallery Liverpool

1997

Rachel Whiteread (exhibition catalogue, essays by Rosalind Krauss, Bartomeu Marí, Stuart Morgan and Michael Tarantino), Palacio de Velázquez, Museo Nacional Centro de Arte Reina Sofia, Madrid

Rachel Whiteread: British Pavilion XLVII Venice Biennale 1997 (exhibition catalogue, interviewed by Andrea Rose), British Council, London

1998

Claustrophobia (exhibition catalogue, edited by Claire Doherty), Ikon Gallery, Birmingham

Direcçao: Escultura (Towards Sculpture) (exhibition catalogue, text by Rui Sanches), Centro de Arte Moderna José de Azeredo Perdigao, Lisbon

Displacements (exhibition catalogue, essays by Jessica Bradley and Andreas Huyssen), Art Gallery of Ontario

Real/Life: New British Art (exhibition catalogue, essays by James Roberts and Andrea Rose), Tochigi Prefectural Museum of Fine Arts, Fukuoka Art Museum, Hiroshima City Museum of Contemporary Art, Museum of Contemporary Art, Tokyo and Ashiya City Museum of Art & History, Japan

Thinking Aloud (exhibition catalogue, essay by Nick Groom, interview between Roger Malbert and Richard Wentworth), Kettle's Yard, Cambridge, Cornerhouse, Manchester and Camden Arts Centre, London

Rachel Whiteread (exhibition catalogue, text by A. M. Homes), Anthony d'Offay Gallery, London

1999

'Carving Space: Interview with David Sylvester', *Tate: The Art Magazine*, London, spring

'Remains of the Day' by Robert Storr, *Art in America*, New York, April

'Concrete Poetry' by Jane Burton, *ARTnews*, New York, May

Looking Up: Rachel Whiteread's Water Tower (ed.) Louise Neri, Scalo and Public Art Fund, New York

2000

Sincerely Yours (exhibition catalogue, text by Oystein Ustvedt), Astrup Fearnley Museum of Modern Art, Oslo

Judenplatz: Place of Remembrance (essay by Andrea Schlieker), Museum Judenplatz, Vienna

2001

Contemporary Art in Print: The Publications of Charles Booth-Clibborn and his Imprint The Paragon Press 1995–2000 (text by Patrick Elliott), London

PHOTOGRAPHIC CREDITS

All works by Rachel Whiteread are reproduced
by courtesy of the owners and the artist. The
photographs have been supplied by Anthony
d'Offay Gallery, London.

© Carl Andre/VAGA, New York/DACS, London,
2001, p.21

Mike Bruce at Gate Studio, London, p.18, cat.9

John Davies, p.19

Gautier Deblonde, p.64

Marian Harders, p.62

Werner Kaligofsky, p.60

Volker Naumann, cat.5

© Tate, London 2001 cat.5 and p.21

Marcus Taylor, cat.1